Can Archaeology Prove the Old Testament?

Ralph O. Muncaster

HARVEST HOUSE PUBLISHERS
Eugene, Oregon 97402

Cover by Terry Dugan Design, Minneapolis, Minnesota

A special thanks to Dr. Rex Moody, archaeological researcher, for his help in corroborating archaeological evidence and findings.

By Ralph O. Muncaster

Are There Hidden Codes in the Bible?

Can You Trust the Bible?

Creation vs. Evolution

Creation vs. Evolution Video

Does the Bible Predict the Future?

How Do We Know Jesus Is God?

Is the Bible Really a Message from God?

Can Archaeology Prove the New Testament?

Can Archaeology Prove the Old Testament?

Science—Was the Bible Ahead of Its Time?

What Is the Proof for the Resurrection?

What Really Happened Christmas Morning?

What Really Happens When You Die?

CAN ARCHAEOLOGY PROVE THE OLD TESTAMENT?
Copyright © 2000 by Ralph O. Muncaster
Published by Harvest House Publishers
Eugene, Oregon 97402

Library of Congress Cataloging-in-Publication Data

Muncaster, Ralph O.
    Can Archaeology Prove the Old Testament? / Ralph O. Muncaster.
        p. cm. — (Examine the evidence series)
    ISBN 0-7369-0356-9
        1. Bible. O.T.—Antiquities. 2. Bible. O.T.—Evidences, authority, etc. I. Title.

BS621 .M84 2000
221.9′3—dc21
                                                                    00-024148

Contents

Is the Old Testament Historically Accurate?

Does it matter?

The Bible presents itself as fact. In matters of history, it claims to present historical fact. In communication from God (that is, prophecy, instruction, or judgment), it also claims to be factual. In order to trust the Bible, it's important to be able to trust that it is accurate and true.

The Bible is *unique* among holy books in that it *commands* its readers to "test everything" (1 Thessalonians 5:21). Does that mean "test" the Bible itself, as well? In a sense, yes—at least to the point of knowing that it is truly inspired by God. Once we realize God has inspired the Bible, we can trust even the difficult-to-understand parts, since God would not make mistakes.

Why would the Bible command us to perform such a test? Very simply, to *set itself apart from other books claiming to be from God*. "Blind faith" can lead people to trust in the wrong source for truth.

Other holy books claim to be historical—but without giving evidence of it. Or they claim to be divinely inspired—without real "proof" of inspiration (for example, without the evidence of fulfilled prophecy). Emotional techniques sometimes use "feelings" that are claimed to be evidence. Or a religion might use philosophical arguments to claim its holy book is true. But if something is *really from God,* wouldn't it be accurate? The Bible is. Wouldn't God provide evidence of His authorship? The Bible does. It contains historical evidence demonstrated to be fact; it is translated from reliable manuscripts; and it provides a trustworthy guide for archaeology. Evidence for divine authorship is also abundant in the Bible, with hundreds of fulfilled prophecies, scientific insights, and examples of concealed evidence.

The accuracy of the Old Testament is vital to the Bible's message:

1. It reveals the power, nature, and expectations of God.

2. It demonstrates our need for a Savior.

3. It defines God's plan of redemption.

4. It verifies the Bible's divine inspiration (by perfect, precise prophecy).

5. It promises the coming of Jesus Christ.

6. It confirms Jesus as the Messiah (through perfectly fulfilled prophecy).

Archaeology provides one means of confirming the historical accuracy of the Bible. Only a century ago, some people thought

modern archaeology would prove the Bible false. Instead, investigation has verified many of its historical accounts to the smallest detail. Some of the Bible's greatest skeptics have now become its greatest supporters. And the Bible is routinely used as an archaeological resource.

The Foundational Issues

If God inspired the Bible, it would be accurate. Does history confirm this?

It goes without saying that if the God who created the universe inspired His selected authors for the purpose of communicating with us, then His Scripture would be accurate. Evidence from history, however, is different from other types of evidence.

1. What Is the General Nature of Historical Evidence?

Analytical evidence is used to prove things that exist by definition (for example, 2+2=4 and other mathematical and scientific calculations).

Statistical evidence is used to prove events in reference to probability (for example, the probability that someone would win the lottery, or that Jesus and prophecy about the Messiah are interrelated).

Legal evidence is used to confirm historical events (for example, that Alexander the Great conquered Israel, or that Julius Caesar or the events of the Bible are real).

Therefore, it is impossible to "prove" any historical fact in the same sense that we can prove mathematical equations—or define an extremely probable event as proven. In history, we have available only eyewitness testimony (written and verbal) and circumstantial evidence (these are the same types of evidence relied upon in our legal system).

2. Do We Have Reliable Historical Evidence for the Bible?

There is more historical evidence for the Bible, by far, than for any other historical chronicle. This evidence is apparent in the vast number and reliability of the manuscripts of the Bible and in the archaeological findings that support the biblical accounts of events (see pages 22–45).

3. What Does the Historical Evidence for the Bible Mean?

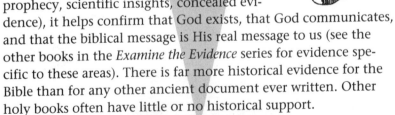

The "legal" evidence (from archaeology and manuscripts) concurs with the claims of the Bible. It can't "prove" that events happened. But it does provide the Bible with the highest degree of credibility available. When the legal evidence is used together with other evidence of communication from God in the Bible (for example, prophecy, scientific insights, concealed evidence), it helps confirm that God exists, that God communicates, and that the biblical message is His real message to us (see the other books in the *Examine the Evidence* series for evidence specific to these areas). There is far more historical evidence for the Bible than for any other ancient document ever written. Other holy books often have little or no historical support.

How the Bible Fits with History

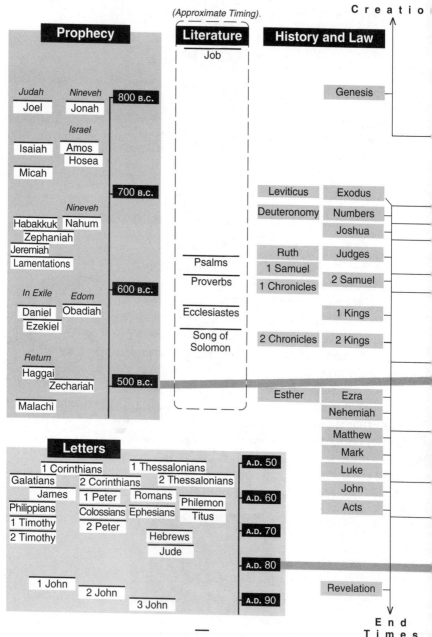

(Approximate Timing).

Creatio

Prophecy

Literature

History and Law

Job

| Judah | Nineveh | 800 B.C. |
| Joel | Jonah | |

Genesis

Israel

Isaiah | Amos
Micah | Hosea

700 B.C.

Leviticus | Exodus

Deuteronomy | Numbers

Joshua

Nineveh
Habakkuk | Nahum
Zephaniah
Jeremiah
Lamentations

Psalms

Ruth | Judges
1 Samuel
1 Chronicles | 2 Samuel

Proverbs

600 B.C.

In Exile | Edom
Daniel | Obadiah
Ezekiel

Ecclesiastes

1 Kings

Song of Solomon

2 Chronicles | 2 Kings

Return
Haggai
Zechariah

500 B.C.

Malachi

Esther | Ezra

Nehemiah

Matthew

Letters

Mark

Luke

1 Corinthians | 1 Thessalonians | A.D. 50
Galatians | 2 Corinthians | 2 Thessalonians
James | 1 Peter | Romans | Philemon | A.D. 60
Philippians | Colossians | Ephesians | Titus
1 Timothy | 2 Peter
2 Timothy

John

Acts

Hebrews | A.D. 70
Jude

A.D. 80

1 John
2 John

Revelation

3 John | A.D. 90

8

End
Times

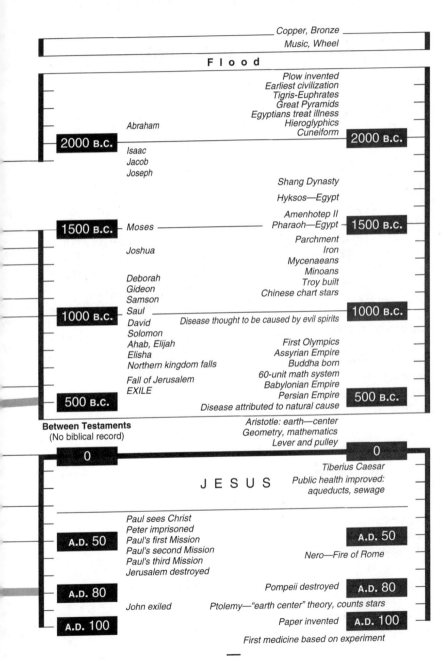

Copper, Bronze
Music, Wheel

F l o o d

Plow invented
Earliest civilization
Tigris-Euphrates
Great Pyramids
Egyptians treat illness
Abraham   Hieroglyphics
Cuneiform

2000 B.C.   **2000 B.C.**

Isaac
Jacob
Joseph

Shang Dynasty

Hyksos—Egypt

Amenhotep II
1500 B.C. — Moses ———— Pharaoh—Egypt **1500 B.C.**

Parchment
Joshua   Iron
Mycenaeans
Minoans
Deborah   Troy built
Gideon   Chinese chart stars
Samson

1000 B.C. — Saul ———————————————— **1000 B.C.**
David   Disease thought to be caused by evil spirits
Solomon
Ahab, Elijah   First Olympics
Elisha   Assyrian Empire
Northern kingdom falls   Buddha born
   60-unit math system
Fall of Jerusalem   Babylonian Empire
EXILE   Persian Empire
500 B.C.   Disease attributed to natural cause   **500 B.C.**

Between Testaments   Aristotle: earth—center
(No biblical record)   Geometry, mathematics
Lever and pulley

0   **0**

Tiberius Caesar
J E S U S   Public health improved:
aqueducts, sewage

Paul sees Christ
Peter imprisoned
A.D. 50 — Paul's first Mission   **A.D. 50**
Paul's second Mission
Paul's third Mission   Nero—Fire of Rome
Jerusalem destroyed

Pompeii destroyed
A.D. 80   **A.D. 80**
John exiled   Ptolemy—"earth center" theory, counts stars

Paper invented   **A.D. 100**
A.D. 100

First medicine based on experiment

Old Testament History and Archaeology

The Book of Genesis

Genesis relates the beginning of mankind in the garden of Eden and the lives of Adam, Eve, and their descendants. While it would be inconceivable to have specific archaeological support for the existence of the family of Adam, we do have indications of the earliest culture in the area associated with the Garden of Eden (see page 24).

The flood of Noah is described in detail in the Bible—and virtually every culture in every part of the world has ancient accounts of a great flood destroying life and of the saving of one family. Some accounts even contain names similar to Noah (see page 25). Furthermore, there are quite a few people who believe the actual ark of Noah exists under a periodically receding glacier on Mount Ararat in Turkey. Evidence cited includes writings of Marco Polo, photographs, and testimonies. Archaeology has yet to confirm or deny this.

Archaeology has uncovered evidence of "tower-of-Babel" structures (ziggurats—see page 25). One destroyed ziggurat that has the characteristics described in the Bible is thought by some people to be the actual remains of the tower of Babel. Scholars also have determined that all languages of the world originated from a common language in the region of Mesopotamia.

The Earliest Biblical Writing

The earliest portion of the Bible may have been actually written down as early as the time of Abraham (about 2000 B.C.). The events of Job are believed to have occurred about Abraham's time in Mesopotamia—an area where writing was well developed. Abraham's hometown of Ur was a center of education. Clay tablets have been discovered in Ur that recorded various contracts, teaching methods, and advanced mathematics. Abraham, who was from a family of wealth, was probably highly educated. It's conceivable that manuscripts of Job (or other records) were passed from Abraham to Moses through Abraham's heirs, though no supporting evidence has been found yet. Animal skins were used to record state documents as early as 3000 B.C., making it possible that Abraham—a nomad—possessed such portable written documents.

The Historical Books of Moses

Moses wrote the first five books of the Bible, which cover creation, the patriarchs, the exodus from Egypt, and God's laws.

Writing at the time of Moses was quite advanced, especially in Egypt. Hieroglyphics were often written on parchment—a specially prepared animal skin that was more durable than papyrus (a paper-like substance made of reeds from the Nile). Moses, educated in the best Egyptian schools, would certainly have had the ability to write.

Moses Confirmed as Author

In the 1800s, scholars who followed the methods of "higher criticism" believed that Moses could not have written the first five books of the Bible since, they argued, written culture had not developed adequately to create such a *system* of laws. In 1902 the Code of Hammurabi was discovered (see page 31). A record of law in Babylon prior to 1750 B.C., when discovered it verified that even other cultures had advanced systems of writing and law. "Higher criticism" also claimed that the use of different "names" of God in the *Torah* (the first five books of the Bible) was evidence of different authors for the different books. Substantial modern research has soundly refuted that idea as well. The Bible, and Jesus Himself, clearly indicate Moses' authorship of the Torah (see Exodus 24:4; Deuteronomy 31:9; Mark 10:5, 12:19; Luke 20:28; John 1:45, 5:46).

Other Books of History

Other historical books—Joshua, Judges, Ruth, Samuel, Kings, Chronicles, Esther, Nehemiah, and Ezra—were written by scribes, whose duty was to maintain the holy record.

The Book of Joshua covers the period of Joshua's leadership from his call by God, through the entrance into Canaan and his victory over Jericho, to the conquering of much of the land. The Book of Judges continues the history of Israel, describing how the nation fell into apostasy, faced defeats by enemies, and was repeatedly restored by judges called by God (for example, Deborah, Gideon, and Samson). Ruth provides added understanding of the interaction of Israel with neighboring cultures (Ruth was a Moabite) and gives valuable insight into the role of the "kinsman-redeemer"—a role-type eventually fulfilled by Christ. The books of Samuel cover the period from Judges through the beginning of the monarchy (through David). The books of Kings continue the history from King Solomon through the fall of Jerusalem and into the time of the exile in Babylon.

The books of Chronicles overlap books of history from Noah to the fall of Jerusalem. Written centuries later, the Chronicles provide a slightly different perspective than other historical books. They were the last Old Testament books to be officially recognized (canonized). The books of Ezra, Nehemiah, and Esther all deal with the history of the Israelites after their exile to Babylon. Ezra and Nehemiah focus on the return to and rebuilding of Jerusalem. Esther describes the provision of God to those who did not return.

The Books of Wisdom Literature

Although Job—written about 2000 B.C.—is considered a book of literature, and some Psalms were written as early as the time of Moses or as late as 400 B.C., most of the books of literature were written about 1000 B.C. The key authors were King Solomon, who wrote Proverbs, Ecclesiastes, and Song of Songs; and David, who wrote most of the Psalms. Literary books were regarded as Scripture quite early.

The wisdom literature deals more with feelings, attitudes, and wisdom, and less with historical events. So it's no surprise that archaeological discoveries lend credibility to these books *indirectly* (for instance, through evidence of culture, rather than through identification of specific historical events). Even so, most of the content of the wisdom literature can be traced to specific historical events, or at least placed in a historical context.

The Books of Prophecy

As with the books of history, most of the books of prophecy are believed to have been written by scribes of the prophets, or sometimes by the prophets themselves. Prophecy was *extremely important* to the people of Israel and was regarded as a vital test of "someone speaking for God." Hence, whenever a prophet spoke in the name of God (that is, "Thus saith the Lord"), it was deemed to be "of God"; and the consequences were very serious if the prophecy did not come true. If a prophecy did not come true, the law commanded that the false prophet be *put to death*.

Is Absence of Evidence Evidence of Absence?

Some people say, "No evidence means it didn't exist." So far, no patriarch name inscriptions previous to Moses have been found on any clay tablets. But we *should not expect* to find such records. The patriarchs were nomads of little or no world acclaim, not kings building pyramids. Even so, many other ancient writings *do* cite biblical events and people (for example, Islam's Qur'an).

Consequently, the content of the books of prophecy had to be *100-percent accurate* for them to qualify as books of prophecy. Not surprisingly, these books have proven to be entirely accurate when studied from the perspective of archaeology.

The Israelites, who wrote the Old Testament, made little distinction between the books of prophecy and the books of history. In fact, the Jews originally (as they do today) placed many books we call history in the category of prophecy (Joshua, Judges, Samuel, and Kings). Others are grouped as part of "the writings" (Esther, Ezra-Nehemiah, and Chronicles). To the Jews, history and prophecy were inextricably intertwined. History could be documented and was commonly recorded by many cultures. Prophecy, however, was *Israel's assurance* that the writings were *from God* (because only God can foretell the future—see Isaiah 46:10). Hence, the short-term prophecy contained in the Old Testament gave the Jews confidence that the writings were actual Scripture—inspired by God. It helped them sort out the Old Testament from other historical writings. The longer-term prophecies—those fulfilled by Christ—give us the same confidence today. In other words, how would Old Testament prophets know in advance the many details of Jesus' life without inspiration from God?

Archaeological evidence for the books of prophecy includes names, sites, events, and considerable evidence of cultural practices at the time. The sites of evidence are controlled by the Jews or neighboring Arab nations (Palestine), and also by the modern-day or nations in the areas where the Jews were slaves (Egypt) or held captive (Babylon).

Intertestament History

After the rebuilding of Jerusalem following the exile, the Bible is silent for about 400 years. The New Testament resumes the chronological record with the birth of Christ. Other historical accounts provide insight into this period. The writings of Josephus (see page 45) and the apocryphal books (see *Can You Trust the Bible?* in the *Examine the Evidence* series) are two examples.

Persia exercised political control over Palestine (under Darius I, II and III; Xerxes; Artaxerxes I, II and III; and others) until Alexander the Great started the mighty campaign that resulted in his conquest of a vast region extending from India to Macedonia to Egypt. Palestine was conquered by Alexander in 334 B.C. Many archaeological findings confirm the events surrounding and the influence of Alexander the Great.

The impact of Greece in this period (the Hellenistic period) far outlasted Alexander's control. In addition to many cultural changes, the common language of Palestine became *Koine* Greek—the language used to write most of the New Testament.

Greek quickly became somewhat of a universal language, as English is today. The impact of Greek was so strong that eventually Jews "lost" the language of ancient Hebrew. Because of the need for the Jews to understand Scripture, the entire Old Testament and the books of the Apocrypha were translated from Hebrew into Greek in about 280–250 B.C. This work was done in the great cultural center of Alexandria, Egypt, which had been founded by Alexander the Great. This famous translation is called the Septuagint, and it is still widely referenced today.

Control of Palestine after Alexander's death in 323 B.C. soon changed hands with a division of his kingdom (301 B.C.) which allocated much of the previously Persian area to Seleucus and much of the Egyptian area to Ptolemy. Struggles for control of Palestine between the two dynasties continued until the hated Seleucid king Antiochus IV Epiphanes was defeated by the Jews in the Maccabean revolt in 165 B.C. Antiochus IV was especially hated because of his decrees to prevent the Jews from worshiping, which reached their worst when he sacrificed a pig (a forbidden animal) on the altar of the Lord in 168 B.C. (called the "abomination of desolation" in the Book of Daniel). Exactly three years later to the day (the twenty-fifth day of the ninth Jewish month—about December), Judas Maccabaeus, leader of the revolt, captured the temple. The anniversary of that event is celebrated as Hanukkah.

The final period prior to Roman control (the Hasmonean period, 165–32 B.C.) was the last period of Jewish rule until Israel became a nation in 1947. The Romans, building their empire, considered the Hasmoneans a good counterbalance to the weakening Seleucid Empire. Many archaeological findings support the nonbiblical accounts written from 400 B.C. to the time of Christ.

Today there is a vast quantity of archaeological evidence—from literally millions of discoveries—supporting every book of the Bible. Because of this, many non-Christians agree with biblical history. This booklet contains only a *very small portion* of the available evidence. Even more significant is the fact that only a tiny fraction of known biblical sites have ever been excavated. Modern archaeology proceeds at a slow, methodical pace, and funding and staff for the work are highly limited.

How Archaeology Is Conducted

Modern archaeology is highly organized and meticulous, keeps records in depth, and is *very* slow. Centuries ago "treasure hunters" obliterated many sites in search of quick riches. Today, archaeologists value most writings and artifacts more than gold or gems.

In the Middle East, the common form of a site for excavation is a large mound, called a *tell*, which is essentially a buried city. Tells usually span several cultures. Throughout history, building sites were carefully selected, based on such things as water supply and natural defense. When a city was conquered and destroyed, it was typical for the victors to rebuild on top of the old city. As time passed, this cycle of destruction and rebuilding resulted in a large man-made hill. Of course, the uppermost level represented the most recent civilization, the lower ones earlier cultures. Occasionally pits were dug through several strata.

As excavation takes place, the precise location and relationship of various artifacts is lost forever. Therefore, digs are systematically divided into square areas and frequently photographed. Each artifact is thoroughly documented. Digging may start with shovels, which as critical areas are approached are quickly replaced with small hand tools—even spoons and toothbrushes. Because of the enormous time and expense required, only a small dent has been made to date in the tens of thousands of potential sites.

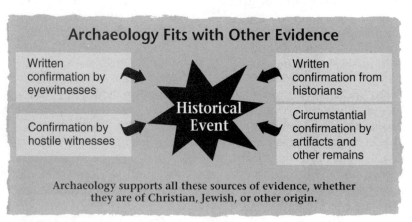

Archaeology Fits with Other Evidence

Written confirmation by eyewitnesses

Written confirmation from historians

Confirmation by hostile witnesses

Historical Event

Circumstantial confirmation by artifacts and other remains

Archaeology supports all these sources of evidence, whether they are of Christian, Jewish, or other origin.

How Archaeological Dates Are Determined

Seldom do people leave behind inscriptions of dates or valuable dated materials, such as coins. However, the vast amount of pottery left behind—with obvious style changes that can be referenced to dates—provides an abundant and reliable source of dating. As an example, the oil lamps below show a very distinct progression of style readily recognizable by archaeologists. Such lamps are very commonly found in the Holy Lands.[8]

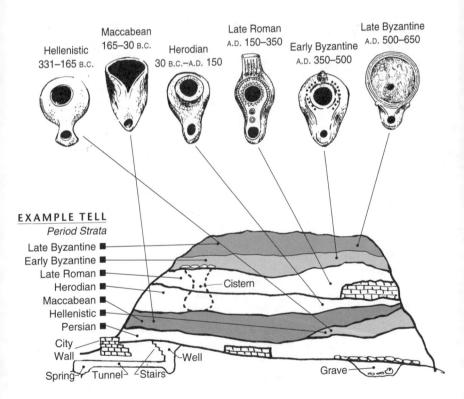

Hellenistic
331–165 B.C.

Maccabean
165–30 B.C.

Herodian
30 B.C.–A.D. 150

Late Roman
A.D. 150–350

Early Byzantine
A.D. 350–500

Late Byzantine
A.D. 500–650

EXAMPLE TELL
Period Strata

Late Byzantine ■
Early Byzantine ■
Late Roman ■
Herodian ■
Maccabean ■
Hellenistic ■
Persian ■

City Wall
Spring Tunnel Stairs Well

Cistern

Grave

Archaeology—a New Science

It's natural to think of archaeology as an "old science." After all, it involves old things. Most people are surprised to learn that archaeology is relatively new, whether or not it is really a "science." (Some people define "science" as only the disciplines using the scientific method. Others broaden it to include almost all areas of systematic fact-finding.)

Archaeology is the systematic study of things that cultures have left behind. It was not a subject of professional interest until the 1700s. At that time it focused primarily on "valuable" objects (mainly gold and silver artifacts). The systematic (scientific) approach wasn't widely used until the 1900s—years after some critics blindly (and incorrectly) assumed the Bible lacked any evidence to support it. In the late 1800s, "higher criticism" (popular at the time) suggested the Bible might be full of myths and errors. Some archaeologists sought to "prove" the Bible to be inaccurate. Others took the opposite approach and attempted to find evidence for it. The Bible archaeologists working in the Middle East were surprised at their discoveries, which supported the Bible in virtually all details (see insert on "Great Archaeologists"). Some other archaeologists, who searched the Americas for evidence of other holy books (for example, the Book of Mormon, written in the 1800s) found no evidence and began refocusing on early American Indian cultures.

Using the Bible as a guide, archaeologists began finding parts of history they didn't know existed. Ancient cultures thought to be nonexistent were discovered. Ancient cities thought to be myths were found. And events thought to be "legends" were confirmed. Today the Bible is regarded as a fundamental archaeological reference.

We should realize, however, that most of this archaeological evidence has appeared in the *last 50 years*. Only since half a century ago have discoveries uncovered strong evidence for the existence of cities such as Sodom and Gomorrah, people as prominent as King David, or cultures such as the early Hittites. Now museums are filled with archaeological evidence supporting the Bible.

Yet many textbooks and much public opinion are still based on remnants of the inaccurate period of "higher criticism" from the 1800s to the early 1900s. Unfortunately, it takes time to correct long-standing misconceptions.

Great Archaeologists Switch to the Bible

Old Testament: *William Albright*—As a young man, Albright regarded the Bible as simply a book of literature not based on historical fact. He intended to use archaeology to define how such "literature" fit within the cultural framework of the time. During his field studies in the 1930s (which continued until his death in 1971), Albright found conclusive evidence that caused him to reverse his previous position. He proclaimed that the Bible was, in fact, *totally consistent with archaeological findings.*

New Testament: *William Ramsay*—Ramsay set out to disprove the Gospel of Luke in the late nineteenth century. After 30 years of in-depth archaeology in Asia Minor and the Middle East, Ramsay's conclusions were the opposite of his initial premise. The academic world was shocked. Expecting historical proof against the Bible, instead it was presented with strong confirmation of biblical accuracy. Ramsay called Luke one the greatest historians ever—and he converted to Christianity based on his research.

Key Sites of Palestine

Beersheba—Tribe of Simeon, southern border of David's empire—Edom to the south

Bethel—Referenced more in Bible than any site except Jerusalem

Damascus—Capital of Syria; oldest continuously inhabited city in the world

Dan—Tribe of Dan; often used to define northern border of Israel

Ezion-geber—Site of important port city built by Solomon (1 Kings 9:26; 10:22)

Gaza—Philistine stronghold, captured by Solomon, punished for sin (Amos 1:6,7)

Gezer—Captured by Joshua (Joshua 10:33; 12:12), later lost to Philistines

Hazor—Large size and strategic location—one of Joshua's key cities (Joshua 11:10)

Hebron—Highest city in Israel—key city for Abraham (Genesis 13:18; 23:19); site of patriarchs' graves

Jericho—Maybe oldest city in the world; stronghold—first captured by Joshua

Jerusalem—Most important city of Israelites; location of temple

Megiddo—Strategic military stronghold; horse, chariot city of Solomon (1 Kings 9:15-19)

Petra—Spectacular trade city with buildings cut into rocks; narrow entry—easy to defend

Qumran—Isolated home of Essene sect; location of Dead Sea scrolls.

Samaria—Capital of northern kingdom; stronghold, but fell to Assyrians in 722 B.C.

Shechem—Destroyed and rebuilt often; northern kingdom capital before Samaria

Succoth—Key city of Jacob after he left Esau (Genesis 33:17); punished by Gideon

Sidon—Oldest and key Phoenician trade city; founded by son of Canaan (Genesis 10:15)

Sodom and Gomorrah—Wicked cities of the plain—destroyed by God (Genesis 19); modern site: Bab edh-Dhra

Tyre—Became greatest Phoenician trade city; conquered by Alexander the Great

Ugarit—Important archaeological site; provides key Old Testament insights into culture, language

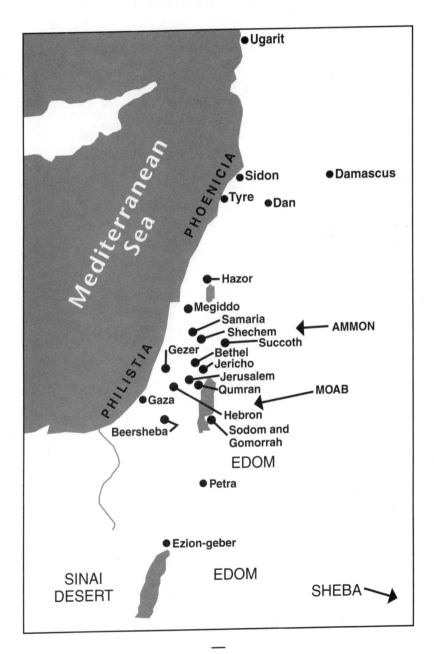

Archaeological Evidence . . .

1. JERICHO 10,000 B.C.
Oldest "known" city •
Tower dated to 8000 B.C. •
Walls tumbled to Joshua •

2. NINEVEH 3100–612 B.C.
Babylon flood—clay tablets •
Capital of Assyrian empire •
Jonah prophesied there •

3. UR 4500–1900 B.C.
Ziggurats like tower of Babel •
Abraham's hometown •
Advanced Amorite capital •

4. MARI 2500–1700 B.C.
Strong Amorite city •
20,000 clay tablets—treaties •
Trades with cities in Canaan •

5. BABYLON 2300 B.C.
Ziggurat-like tower of Babel •
Nebuchadnezzar, exile of Jews •
Birthplace of pagan religions •

6. JERUSALEM 2200 B.C.
Cited in Egyptian hieroglyphics •
Abraham and Melchizedek (Salem) •
Most important biblical city •

7. EBLA 2500–400 B.C.
Thousands of cuneiform tablets •
Language similar to Hebrew •
Sargon conquered •

8. MEGIDDO 4200 B.C.
Conquered by Egyptians—1468 B.C. •
Solomon's horse stables found •
Site of Shishak's victory stele •

9. SUSA 2000 B.C.
Code of Hammurabi found •
Capital of Elamites, Persians •
Home of Nehemiah, Artaxerxes •

10. HATTUSA 1900–1200 B.C.
Hittite capital •
10,000 cuneiform tablets found •
Treaty with Egypt, kings' names •

11. EGYPT 3100 B.C.
Artwork of early Hebrews found •
Cultural ties to Israelites •
Evidence of Egyptians in Israel •

12. UGARIT 2000–1200 B.C.
Thousands of cuneiform tablets •
Language similar to Hebrew •
Findings of Baal, pagan gods •

13. SAMARIA 2500–400 B.C.
Founded by Omri •
Capital of region of Samaria •
Capital of northern kingdom •

14. QUMRAN 2500–400 B.C.
Hundreds of Dead Sea scrolls •
All Old Testament except Esther •
Cultural insight of Essenes •

. . . of the Old Testament (A small sample of discoveries to date)

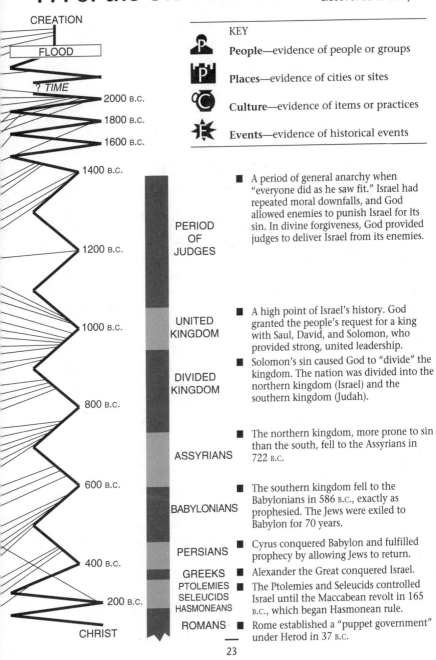

CREATION

FLOOD

? TIME

2000 B.C.

1800 B.C.

1600 B.C.

1400 B.C.

1200 B.C.

1000 B.C.

800 B.C.

600 B.C.

400 B.C.

200 B.C.

CHRIST

KEY

People—evidence of people or groups

Places—evidence of cities or sites

Culture—evidence of items or practices

Events—evidence of historical events

PERIOD OF JUDGES

- A period of general anarchy when "everyone did as he saw fit." Israel had repeated moral downfalls, and God allowed enemies to punish Israel for its sin. In divine forgiveness, God provided judges to deliver Israel from its enemies.

UNITED KINGDOM

- A high point of Israel's history. God granted the people's request for a king with Saul, David, and Solomon, who provided strong, united leadership.

DIVIDED KINGDOM

- Solomon's sin caused God to "divide" the kingdom. The nation was divided into the northern kingdom (Israel) and the southern kingdom (Judah).

ASSYRIANS

- The northern kingdom, more prone to sin than the south, fell to the Assyrians in 722 B.C.

BABYLONIANS

- The southern kingdom fell to the Babylonians in 586 B.C., exactly as prophesied. The Jews were exiled to Babylon for 70 years.

PERSIANS

- Cyrus conquered Babylon and fulfilled prophecy by allowing Jews to return.

GREEKS ■ Alexander the Great conquered Israel.

PTOLEMIES SELEUCIDS HASMONEANS

- The Ptolemies and Seleucids controlled Israel until the Maccabean revolt in 165 B.C., which began Hasmonean rule.

ROMANS ■ Rome established a "puppet government" under Herod in 37 B.C.

Ancient Discoveries

Creation to 1900 B.C.

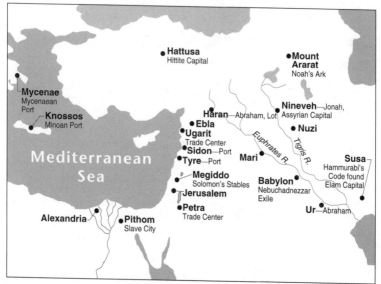

Sites of Old Testament History

The Garden of Eden (Genesis 2)—The Bible provides some clues to the location of the Garden of Eden with its description (Genesis 2:11-14) of four rivers connected in the garden, two of which were the Euphrates and the Hiddekel (now called the Tigris). Current geology indicates this area is most likely in the "fertile crescent" of Mesopotamia.

Cain and Abel (Genesis 4)—One of Cain's family was Jubal, who is the "father of all who play the harp and flute" (4:21). Discoveries at Ur, Abraham's birthplace—not far from the area believed to contain the Garden of Eden—show the earliest evidence of string and wind instruments. Likewise, the Bible says Tubal-cain (another descendant of Cain) was an expert in forging brass and iron (4:22). This formerly seemed to contradict "science," which placed the beginning of the Iron Age as late as 1200 B.C. However, at Tell Asmar (Eshnunna) about 50 miles northwest of Baghdad—again near the probable site of the Garden of Eden—an iron blade was found dating from no later than 2700 B.C., long before the dawn of the Iron Age.

Long Life Spans—People had long life spans—up to 969 years—until the Flood. This is difficult for modern people to comprehend, especially since we see life spans increase so slowly. Scientists studying the biblical claim have discovered possible explanations, one being the explosion of the Vela supernova, which dramatically increased radiation to the earth from space about the time of the Flood. Archaeology has found claims of long life (many thousands of years) for "early kings" in ancient Babylonian clay tablets. While the Babylonian accounts are mythological, it seems people of that era did not regard such long life spans as especially unusual.

The Flood (Genesis 6)—Archaeology has uncovered *more than 200 accounts* from cultures all over the world of a major flood that destroyed humanity and animals. All have parallels to the biblical record. An example is the Babylonian flood account from the library of Ashurbanipal, king of Assyria. Found in Nineveh in 1854, it closely replicates the biblical record, even in details such as the name of Noah, the number of people in the ark, and the releasing of a dove to see when waters were cleared.

The Tower of Babel (Genesis 11)—Many structures, called ziggurats, have been discovered in ancient cities in the region where the Tower of Babel is believed to have existed, and at least two sites have been proposed for the Tower itself. The word *babel* (Hebrew for *Babylon*) means "gateway to God"—in this case, apparently not *the* God. Ziggurats were very high towers containing a shrine at the top. Brick was used in construction, precisely as indicated in the Bible. One fragment of a clay tablet found in Babylon tells of one temple that so "offended the gods" that it was destroyed one night, and the people were scattered with their "speech made strange." This seems to be a pagan account of the biblical event.[2]

P **Abraham's Cities**—Archaeologists believe that from 2400–2000 B.C. cities were declining as people moved into the country. Fewer cities existed, making it easier for Abraham, a nomad, to enter Canaan, a potentially hostile land. At first glance there seems to be a conflict in the account, with cities mentioned that were in ruins at the time of Abraham (for example, Shechem—Genesis 12:6). However, the Bible terms this location the "site" of Shechem. The city had existed before, and its ruins—site—would have borne the same name.[2]

Abraham in Egypt (Genesis 12:10-20)—Archaeologists now support two details of Abraham's sojourn in Egypt that were once thought inaccurate: 1) Asian Semitics were present in the area at the time of Abraham—confirmed by a tomb painting at Beni Hassan in Egypt; and 2) Camels were in the region in Abraham's time—they are depicted on paintings on the walls of the temple of Hatshepsut (near the city of Thebes), which dates back to that period.[2]

P **Sodom and Gomorrah** (Genesis 19)—The cities of the plain may be under shallow water at the south end of the Dead Sea (it fluctuates greatly—37 feet in a few decades). Another site, Bab edh-Dhra, appears to be a possible location of Sodom or Gomorrah. It's located adjacent to a large graveyard showing mass simultaneous burial. Also, a thick layer of ash covers the ruins. Josephus, the first-century historian, records that "traces" of all five cities of the plain were visible at that time.[2, 5]

Gates and Doors—Gates of cities are described in the Bible as important places to conduct business or meet. Cities unearthed that date from Old Testament times reveal that many Palestinian cites had built-in benches at city gates to provide rest to those waiting for other people. Also, since Palestine had become rural during the time of Abraham and Lot, with cities in a state of decline, critics once argued that there was no need of nor evidence for the massive doors described as part of Lot's house (Genesis 19:9,10). However, at Kiriath Sepher, a biblical city in the area, evidence of similar strong walls and massive doors has been found that dates from 2200–1600 B.C., the time of Lot.[2]

Early Hittites (Genesis 15:20; 23:10; 26:34)—"Higher criticism" of the Bible (which was the popular scientific opinion in the late nineteenth century) proclaimed that the Hittites were a myth. Many discoveries since then, along with the subsequent translation of hieroglyphics, provide substantial proof of a large Hittite empire in Syria, with tribal areas extending southward into Canaan. Evidence includes many monuments, the ancient Hittite capital of Hattusa (much larger than Jericho), hundreds of clay tablets, and even a peace treaty with Egypt. So vast is the amount of evidence today that many museums contain Hittite artifacts; and in some universities a Ph.D. can be earned in Hittite studies alone.[2, 6]

Sarah's Grave (Genesis 23)—Abraham's dealings and method of payment (weighing out silver) for Sarah's gravesite have been borne out by archaeological discovery. Minting of coins did not begin until about 800 B.C.

Rocks of Iron, Hills of Copper

God told Moses that the promised land would have "rocks of iron and copper that could be dug from the hills" (Deuteronomy 8:9). Twenty miles south of the Dead Sea, a large area is dotted with ancient furnaces. The vast region is covered with heaps of copper slag, and some copper veins are still visible above ground.

Although the owner Ephron's offer to "give" the tomb to Abraham sounds generous today, it was simply a tactic of bargaining then. In fact, the 400 shekels that Abraham paid was quite a high price—probably about double the tomb's market value.

A cave in Hebron is believed to be the actual grave of Sarah (and of Abraham, Isaac, and Jacob—Genesis 25:9; 49:29,30). Now a Moslem mosque has been built over it (Abraham and Sarah are revered by most Moslems). Although access to the cave has generally been forbidden, at least twice the cave has been entered by non-Moslems (one of whom did not realize its significance). Shortly after the Six-Day War of 1967, a 12-year-old girl was lowered into the cave, some 12 feet underground. A 57-foot corridor led to a blocked entrance, presumably leading to other underground areas. Three large stones, one appearing to be a tombstone, were in front of it. And during World War I, a British officer, looking for other soldiers, slid down an incline into a 20-foot by 20-foot room. He reported a stone object measuring six feet long, three feet wide, and three feet high. Only later did he realize it might have been Sarah's tomb.[2]

Laban's Idols (Genesis 31)—Archaeology can provide insight into events that seem unusual to us today. Jacob worked for Laban for 20 years to receive brides and livestock. Upon leaving, Rachel, a wife of Jacob, stole Laban's idols, placing them in her saddle. Laban looked for the idols, journeying seven days to find Jacob. Jacob—not knowing Rachel had taken them—said he would kill anyone found with the idols. Laban searched everything except Rachel's saddle (she would not dismount, using her monthly cycle as an excuse). Why all the fuss about idols? The Nuzi tablets, discovered in the same area, indicate that a family member possessing such idols could make a claim to an estate. We also know Jacob's wives were concerned about their inheritance (Genesis 31:14). The stolen idols may have been for the purpose of establishing legal claims.

Ancient Discoveries
1900 B.C. to 1100 B.C.

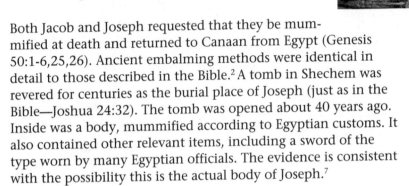

Jacob and Joseph (Genesis 37–50)—Joseph was near the city of Dothan when he was thrown into a well (Genesis 37:17-20). Excavation of Dothan revealed a cistern with several skeletons—indicating wells were used to "dispose" of people in Joseph's day.

Both Jacob and Joseph requested that they be mummified at death and returned to Canaan from Egypt (Genesis 50:1-6,25,26). Ancient embalming methods were identical in detail to those described in the Bible.[2] A tomb in Shechem was revered for centuries as the burial place of Joseph (just as in the Bible—Joshua 24:32). The tomb was opened about 40 years ago. Inside was a body, mummified according to Egyptian customs. It also contained other relevant items, including a sword of the type worn by many Egyptian officials. The evidence is consistent with the possibility this is the actual body of Joseph.[7]

From Leaders to Slaves—Joseph became a prominent leader in Egypt. Yet the Bible tells us that a "new king, who did not know about Joseph, came to power" and forced the rapidly multiplying Hebrews into slavery (Exodus 1:11). Archaeology has verified that foreigners, including Canaanites, achieved prominence in Egypt. One Canaanite was given the title "first speaker of his Majesty", assuming the Egyptian name "Ramses in the temple of Re." Several other examples of Hebrew leaders appear in various writings from about the time of Joseph.[2] Joseph's prominence may have helped such Hebrews gain power.

History reveals that an Asiatic group, the Hyksos, controlled Egypt from about 1730 to about 1570 B.C. Some scholars suggest the leader who "did not know Joseph" may have come in this period, or possibly was the subsequent native Egyptian ruler, Ahmose I. Either possibility fits well with the probable time of Joseph (about 1900 B.C.), allowing ample time for the Hebrews to "multiply" greatly.

P **Hebrew Slaves Build Cities** (Exodus 1:11; 5:13-18)—The actual store cities of Pithom and Rameses have both been located and show artwork on walls depicting Hebrews making bricks, just as in the Bible. Tell el-Maskhuta, on the Nile delta, has inscriptions containing the word *Pi-Tum* (a version of *Pithom*). Also, an illustration of slaves making bricks has been found on the walls of the tomb of Rekhmere (an Egyptian noble). Some of the bricks at the Hebrew building sites were actually found to contain no straw (this was unusual), which may have been due to the Pharaoh's command that the Hebrews were to procure their own straw (Exodus 5:7). The other city, Rameses, is believed to be Tanis, a site excavated in the early 1920s.[2]

Wandering in the Desert (Exodus 15–39)—One would certainly *not* expect any writing on fragile papyrus to survive from the time of Moses. However, writing found in caves in the Sinai is believed to have been done by the Hebrews during the 40 years in the desert. The writings describe many events of the exodus, including the parting of seas, the name of Moses, and the provision of quail (see insert). The factors which best authenticate the writings include: 1) The style of the language—written as if events were happening *at the time*, as opposed to the retelling of a story; and 2) the uniqueness of the language—a combination of an ancient form of Hebrew and Egyptian. It would seem inconceivable to fraudulently concoct such a language "mix," considering that ancient Hebrew had been virtually lost for centuries. While nobody can prove or disprove the writings' actual authenticity, even the ancient historian Diodorus Siculus acknowledged its existence in 10 B.C. It's interesting to note that God had commanded this type of recording (Deuteronomy 27:2-8).[4]

How Many Quail Were in the Desert?

Some people believe the number of quail God provided (Numbers 11:31) seems unrealistic—if they fell three feet deep upon the ground. The Hebrew word for "upon" was the same as the word for "above" (which is used in some translations). If the quail flew three feet *above* the ground, they would have been easy to capture. Ancient writings found in Sinai record such an event; and quail are caught (with nets) in this area even today.

לא תרצח | אנכי ד
לא תנאף | לא יהיה
לא תגנב | לא תשא
לא תענה | זכור את
לא תחמר | כבד את

The Laws of Moses—For years "higher criticism" of the Bible claimed the laws of Moses (in Leviticus) were far too advanced for the period and could not have been written until 500 B.C. or later. Then in 1902, the Laws of Hammurabi[9] were found carved into a seven-foot tall black *stele* from Babylon—discovered in Susa in Elam—radically changing scholars' views. (A *stele* is a stone monument engraved with a written or pictorial commemoration of an event or achievement.) Written in a period hundreds of years prior to Moses, the laws contain evidence that other cultures already had a legal system very similar to the one God gave to Moses. Even many individual laws have striking similarities. Another discovery of tablets in Ras Shamra (in Syria), these written about 1400–1350 B.C., contains sacrificial laws similar to those written down by Moses. Whether these laws were developed from the influence of the laws of Moses or from prior influence by Abraham is not clear. The Bible indicates that Abraham had God-given laws and commands prior to Moses (Genesis 26:5).

The Tabernacle—Materials used in tabernacle construction once were criticized as unavailable to Moses at the time. Modern research shows differently. ***The Tabernacle Covering*** (Exodus 35:7) made of animal hides was earlier said to be of "badger" skin in some translations of the Bible. Further investigation led later translators to more precisely identify the skin as from "sea cows," or more specifically, dugongs—marine animals resembling dolphins, found in abundance in the region. Arabs in the Sinai make sandals from this skin, which is also referred to in Ezekiel 16:10, using the same Hebrew word *(tachash)*. ***The Bronze Laver*** (Exodus 38:8) was made from women's bronze mirrors. Critics have claimed that such mirrors were not available until about 500 B.C. Egyptian discoveries, however, have revealed a very large number of bronze mirrors in sites dating from the time of Moses. The gifts given to the Israelites by the Egyptians would almost certainly have included such mirrors (Exodus 12:35,36). ***The Sevenfold Lampstand*** (Exodus 37:17-24) was also thought by critics to be of a type not created until about 600–500 B.C. Recent evidence from several sites (Tell Beit Mirsim and various tombs at Dothan) shows sevenfold lamps dating back to the period of Moses.[2]

The Fall of Jericho (Joshua 6)—Excavation of part of the ancient city of Jericho shows evidence of the biblical account. Walls were discovered fallen outward, in a way that would allow a rapid "scrambling over the walls" as indicated in the Bible. Even more interesting was the discovery of untouched containers of grain—something highly unusual for a conquered city (God had commanded that the Israelites "keep away" from plunder, except for precious metals).[2] Today, most prominent archaeologists agree that the fall of Jericho was between 1400–1250 B.C.—the time of Joshua.

Joshua's Conquest (Joshua 12:9-24)—A group of letters, the Amarna Tablets, were written by kings of Palestinian and Syrian cities to kings of Egypt about 1400 B.C. (Joshua's time). These tablets confirm the conditions and many events of the time of Joshua. Seven of the letters were written by kings of Jerusalem, and others were from kings of the important seaports of Tyre and Sidon, along with letters from many of the 31 kings that Joshua conquered. Several mention an invasion by the *Habiru* (a derivative of the word "Hebrew").[2]

Cities of the Time of the Judges (Book of Judges)—Many ancient cities from the time of the judges have been uncovered, including Bethel (Judges 1:23-25), Hazor and Debir (1:11), Beth Shan, Megiddo, and Gezer (1:27,29). The Amarna Tablets confirm the Bible's claim that Jerusalem was *not* captured (1:21). In El-Berith evidence was found of the burning of the "house of Berith" about 1150 B.C., precisely in the time of Abimelech as stated in the Bible (9:45,46). Cities of the Philistines (whose existence was once doubted by critics) are just beginning to be uncovered. So far, Philistine artifacts have been found in over 28 sites and five major centers—all located in Palestine. Even the burning of Gibeah has been confirmed (20:8-40).[2]

Ancient Discoveries

1100 B.C. to 930 B.C.

Dagon, God of the Philistines—The Bible tells how the ark of the covenant was captured by the Philistines and placed in front of the statue of their god, Dagon. Twice the statue was discovered fallen facedown in front of the ark the morning after it was set back up (1 Samuel 5:1-4). Many excavations have confirmed the widespread worship of this god (believed to be the father of the god Baal). Findings include a temple of Dagon at Ugarit, mention of him in the Ras Shamra tablets, and two *steles* erected in Dagon's honor. Even today a town outside the modern city of Tel Aviv, Beit Dagan, still preserves the name of this god.[2]

King David; King Saul's Death (1 Samuel, 1 Chronicles, 1 Kings)—Critics once believed the biblical accounts of David as a musician were false since, they argued, the musical instruments David played were not developed until centuries after his time. Modern archaeology has soundly refuted this idea with discoveries of lyres, flutes, harps, and even a double oboe from over a thousand years before David. These discoveries were made in Ur (Abraham's early home), dated as early as 2500 B.C.; in Egypt, dated to 1900 B.C. (when the Hebrews were there); and even in Palestine, dated from 2000 B.C. to the time of David.[2]

Other people argued that King David was a myth—until 1993. In that year, a stone monument fragment was discovered at Tel Dan, near the border of Israel and Syria. The monument, believed to be a victory *stele*, mentions King David and the "House of David," along with words implying a victory by the king of Damascus, Ben-Hadad, who "smote Ijon, and Dan, and Abel-beth-maachah" (1 Kings 15:20).[4,10]

When King Saul, David's predecessor, died in a battle against the Philistines, they hung his corpse on the walls of the city Beth Shan and placed his armor in the temple of Ashtaroth (1 Samuel 31:3-10). Archaeology confirms the existence of the fertility goddess

Ashtaroth and confirms that the city of Beth Shan was destroyed between 1050 and 1000, precisely the time David would likely have retaliated for the insult. [2]

P **David's Conquest of Jerusalem** (2 Samuel 5:6-9; 1 Chronicles 11:4-8)—King David was the first to capture the city of Jerusalem. The Bible says that Joab, David's general, found a secret water system designed to deliver water from a spring outside the city through a tunnel into a cistern that could be reached from inside the city. At night Joab and his men entered the water system, scaled the cistern's wall, and ascended the passageway into the city for a surprise attack. Discoveries by Kathleen Kenyon in her 1960s excavations determined that David indeed took the city in precisely this manner. A spring, tunnel, and shaft system has been found that meets the biblical criteria and is believed to be the one entered by Joab.[2]

P **David's Empire** (2 Samuel 8:1-10)—David extended the empire of the Israelites by defeating the Philistines to the west, the Moabites to the east, the Syrians to the north, and the Edomites to the south. Critical scholars once attempted to reduce the area of David's conquest by arguing that the area of Zobah (2 Samuel 8:3;1 Chronicles 18:3,6) was actually east of the sea of Galilee, not north of Damascus as implied in the Bible. Discoveries by leading archaeologists have now demonstrated conclusively that Zobah ("Subatu" to the Assyrians) was north of Damascus. Hence, David's empire extended from the Gulf of Aqabah in the south to the Hums region in the north. Thus, his son Solomon inherited a vast empire.[2]

P **King Solomon's Anointing** (1 Kings 1:5-7,41-50)—When David anointed Solomon king, it surprised and frightened his rebellious son Adonijah and his supporters, who heard of the anointing by the loud cheering of the people. Recent discoveries about the locations of these two groups of people show the Gihon spring, where Solomon was, to be at the east of Jerusalem, and the spring, at En Rogel, where Adonijah was, to be about 700 yards south. The Gihon spring would have been in earshot of, but not visible from En Rogel. [2]

P **Solomon's Empire** (1 Kings 4:21; 2 Chronicles 9:26)—The existence of the great Assyrian and Egyptian empires, both very powerful during Solomon's reign, make it difficult for some historians to accept the vastness of Solomon's empire. Recent archaeological discoveries reveal that the time of the unified kingdom of Israel—which reached its peak in Solomon's reign—is precisely when Egypt and Assyria went into a period of decline. Other great empires, including the Hittites and the Mycenaeans (sea people from Greece), had already disappeared. The Bible indicates Solomon traded with Hiram, the king of the Phoenician city of Tyre (1 Kings 5:1). A sarcophagus (stone coffin) found in Syria bears the inscription of the name Hiram *(Ahiram)*. The coffin may have either belonged to the king or a relative. (At a minimum it shows the prominence of Hiram's name at the time.) Other evidence contained in the Cyprus Museum in Sardinia shows inscriptions referencing Solomon's relations with the Phoenicians. These inscriptions date back to his reign.[2]

Solomon rebuilt the three cities (1 Kings 9:15) of Gezer (near Jerusalem), Megiddo (near Galilee), and Hazor (north of Galilee). Excavations of all three cities show an identical gate and casement-wall structure and contain pottery dating the building of these structures to Solomon's reign.[3,9]

P **Solomon's City of Horses** (1 Kings 9:19; 2 Chronicles 8:6)—Solomon had entire cities devoted to the stabling of horses. Excavations at Megiddo (north of Jerusalem) uncovered two large stable compounds that could house a total of 450 horses. The stables were constructed in Solomon's reign and used by kings of the northern kingdom until the time of Omri and Ahab—several generations later.[2]

P **The Queen of Sheba Visits Solomon** (1 Kings 10:1,2)—The Bible mentions a visit by the queen of Sheba, whose camels were laden with gold, spices, and precious stones. Critics once argued that domestication of camels did not occur until much later.

However, cuneiform inscriptions about camels were found on the Black Obelisk of Shalmaneser II. Also, a relief image of a rider on a saddled camel was found on a stone sculpture from Halaf. Both indicate the domestication and riding of camels began at least 200 years before Solomon. Other evidence includes many camel statuettes and bones found in Egypt that date back to 3000 B.C. These artifacts indicate that camels probably were used long before Abraham.

While no *direct* reference to the queen of Sheba has yet been found, indirect evidence supports such a visit. Sheba was located in southern Arabia, probably controlling important caravan trade routes and the southern entrance to the Red Sea. Since Solomon controlled a vast fleet of merchant ships, their passage through the queen's sphere of influence would be likely. Excavations at Bethel have produced a clay stamp used to seal bags of cargo (frankincense and myrrh) from the area of Sheba. The stamp is the first artifact found showing a trade connection between Israel and southern Arabia. It was dated to precisely the time of Solomon.[2]

P **Solomon's Ports and Sea Trade** (1 Kings 10:22)— Solomon's extensive trade included a "fleet of trading ships" at "Tarshish." The fleet was used to, among other things, bring gold, silver, ivory, and apes from faraway places. The word *Tarshish*, however, is an Akkadian (Babylonian) word that literally means "refinery." An ancient inscription found in the city of Nora on the island of Sardinia, west of Italy, indicates the city was named Tarshish in Solomon's day. A second ancient inscription found in Esarhaddon, a Phoenician city in the eastern Mediterranean, refers to the city of Tarshish as at the other end of the Mediterranean (again, Sardinia would fit). Solomon traded with the Phoenicians, so it's probable that the "ships of Tarshish" were of a design common at the time—ships that would carry cargo of gold, silver, ivory, apes, and also ore and refined metals.

Ancient Discoveries
930 B.C. to 700 B.C.

Dating of the Kings of Israel—Thanks to the Assyrians, archaeology can confirm the precise dates of the kings of Israel back to the time of Solomon. Excavations have uncovered lists of *all kings of Assyria from 893–666 B.C.* and the dates they took office (the "eponym lists"). The exact years for each can be established by using an eclipse in Nineveh (May–June 763 B.C.—confirmed by astronomers) as a benchmark. The archaeological records of King Shalmaneser III (858–824) discuss the great battle of Qarqar (853 B.C.) and mention King Ahab of Israel. The battle was in the last year of King Ahab's reign. Since the Bible specifies the succession of kings of Israel and the lengths of their reigns, it is easy to establish the dates of each. [2]

King Jeroboam—An inscription found in Megiddo identified Jeroboam, chosen to be the first king of the northern kingdom after the division. (Jeroboam I separated the northern tribes from Rehoboam, who succeeded Solomon—see 1 Kings 12:20). The inscription was actually a seal found in the royal palace with the words, "Belonging to Shema, servant of Jeroboam." (It is possible—but less likely—that this reference was instead to Jeroboam II, who reigned from 782 to 753 B.C.). [2]

Excavations in Dan include a "high place" of worship built during the reign of Jeroboam. This is believed to be one of the places of calf worship that Jeroboam created to encourage people to maintain their allegiance to the northern kingdom, rather than returning to Jerusalem to worship in the temple (and possibly switching allegiance back to Rehoboam of Judah—1 Kings 12:25-33). [2]

Rehoboam, Shishak—The Bible records an invasion from Egypt led by Pharaoh Shishak, who carried off treasures from the temple (1 Kings 14:25,26). This campaign is confirmed by an inscription in the temple of Karnak in Egypt, which shows, among other things, names of many Palestine cities, along with a sculpted relief of the Egyptian god Amon leading rows of Israelites as captives. [2]

Omri's Dynasty—The sixth king of the northern kingdom of Israel ruled for a period of 12 years (in the first six years, leadership was shared with Tibni). His reign was considered so prominent by the neighboring Assyrians that Israel was referred to as "the House of Omri." At the start of his reign, Omri ruled from the same city as his predecessors: Tirzah (excavated at Tell el-Farah). When he gained sole control over Israel, Omri moved the capital city to a hill which became Samaria—a city he founded (1 Kings 16:23,24). The massive building projects started by Omri were completed after his death by his son, King Ahab. The prophet Elijah started his ministry during Omri's reign and continued it (eventually with the help of Elisha) through a succession of several kings. Samaria, a strong, well-fortified city, remained the capital of the northern kingdom until its conquest by the Assyrians in 722 B.C. [2]

Samaria—Excavation of the city of Samaria has revealed considerable evidence of the kings of the northern kingdom, from Omri through Ahab and other kings, until Samaria's conquest by the Assyrians in the ninth year of King Hoshea's reign (2 Kings 17:6). Within the palace, or "ivory house" (1 Kings 22:39; Amos 3:15), archaeologists discovered some 500 plaques or fragments of ivory used for inlaid decoration of furniture and walls. A large courtyard pool was found and is believed to be the place where King Ahab's blood was washed from his chariot after he was killed in battle (1 Kings 22:38). An abundance of pottery has inscriptions of everyday life, including administrative records of trade with other kingdoms.[2,12]

King Ahab—Evidence of Ahab's reign exists outside of Israel (in neighboring Moab) on a black victory *stele* set up by Moab's King Mesha, recording his victory over Ahab in about 860 B.C. King Ahab married Jezebel (1 Kings 16:31) and began extensive worship of Baal—confirmed by the many seals and inscriptions of the period found in excavations.[2]

King Jehu—The Black Obelisk of Shalmaneser II was discovered in Nimrud, a city just south of Nineveh. One panel depicts

Jehu bowing to King Shalmaneser II of Assyria. An inscription reads, "Tribute of Jehu, son of Omri." Jehu was several kings removed from Omri (he ruled more than 30 years later). This shows the high esteem Assyrians held for Omri (see previous page).[2]

Amos's Prophecy—Amos openly criticized the dishonesty and decadent living of the people of Samaria. He described the Samarians as people who rested on "beds inlaid with ivory" and who "drank wine by the bowlful" and used the "finest lotions" (Amos 6:4-6). Many pieces of ivory from such beds—which often depicted Egyptian gods—have been recovered in Samaria. Discoveries have also revealed several inscriptions of payments of taxes to the royal treasury made in wine and expensive oils. Amos also prophesied the eventual destruction by the Lord of the "winter and summer" house (Amos 3:15). Archaeology has confirmed that winter and summer houses were common at that time. One inscription found at Shamal (Syria) indicated that the royalty had three palaces, including a winter and summer house.[2]

King Menahem and Tiglath-Pileser III (or Pul)—The sixteenth king of Israel, Menahem, paid tribute to Pul, king of Assyria (2 Kings 15:19). Later, the Bible ties the names Pul and Tiglath-Pileser III together (1 Chronicles 5:26). Hebrew studies indicate that both names were used to identify the same king. Clay tablets dating to the time of Pul's reign indicate that both names referred to the same person, and further clarify the reason for the two names, which was to appease Babylon after it was annexed by Assyria (the king allowed the Babylonians to refer to him by a separate name).[2]

Sargon—The Bible mentions Sargon only once: as the king of Assyria who captured Ashdod (Isaiah 20:1). The lack of reference to Sargon in the Bible and elsewhere caused many critics to doubt his existence, until the great palace of Sargon was found 12 miles north of Nineveh. This site has yielded an abundance of priceless items defining Sargon's reign and the culture. Even a specific reference to the attack on Ashdod was found in Sargon's records, where he states, "Azuru, king of Ashdod, plotted in his heart to withhold tribute and sent [messages] of hostility to the kings round about him. Against Ashdod, his royal city, I advanced in haste. Ashdod, Gimtu [Gath], and Asdudimmu, I besieged, I captured."[2]

Isaiah's Criticism of Vain Women (Isaiah 3:16-24)— Isaiah warned Israel that its sinfulness was the reason for attacks by enemies—the attacks were a result of God's judgment. He criticized the women of the day for their vanity, flirting, "sweet smell," and overindulgence in cosmetics. Excavations at Kiriath Sepher reveal an extent of cosmetic usage that would rival the most extreme usage today. Vanity palettes were found in such great abundance that it appeared all females used them extensively.[2]

God's Protection of Jerusalem (2 Kings 19:20-36)—Isaiah prophesied that God would protect Jerusalem against attack by Sennacherib of Assyria. An angel of the Lord killed 185,000 Assyrians the night after the prophecy (Isaiah 37:35,36). Excavation of two separate cylinders (the Taylor cylinder from ancient Nineveh and the Oriental Institute cylinder) both confirm this unusual event, stating with great pride the defeats of many cities in Palestine, yet acknowledging the failure to conquer Jerusalem.[2]

Hezekiah's Tunnel (2 Kings 20:20; 2 Chronicles 32:30)— Hezekiah built a conduit to bring more water into the city from the spring Gihon, in order to provide for the event of a siege by the Assyrians. This 1880-foot-long, six-foot-high tunnel ended at the Pool of Siloam, where an inscription was found that described how workers started at each end and "could hear each other digging" as they finally met in the middle (*without* the benefit of modern engineering).[2]

Ancient Discoveries
700 B.C. to the Time of Christt

Deuteronomy Found by Josiah's High Priest (2 Kings 22:5-8)—Archaeologists have shed some light on the finding of "the Book of Law" (Deuteronomy) during King Josiah's reign. In ancient times, important writings were often placed in the cornerstones of buildings. It seems likely that workers uncovered the writings while making repairs.[2]

The Exile (2 Kings, Daniel, Ezekiel)—There is substantial archaeological evidence of three separate phases in the exile of Judah to Babylon. The first (605 B.C.), when Daniel was deported, is confirmed by the "Babylon Chronicle," found in the court records of Babylon. The second (597 B.C.), when Ezekiel was captured, is confirmed by the "Chronicles of the Chaldean Kings." And the third and final deportation, following the fall of Jerusalem (586 B.C.), is supported by the "Lachish Letters."[2]

The Dead Sea Scrolls—The most important archaeological find in history is probably that of the Dead Sea scrolls. About one-third of the hundreds of scrolls are of the Old Testament (copies, often multiples, of every book except Esther), many written at least a century or two before Christ. The remaining scrolls contain a vast amount of information about the culture of the period. Hidden in jars in caves up to A.D. 70 and then forgotten until 1947, the scrolls are like a time capsule, showing virtually no difference from today's Masoretic text (see *Can You Trust the Bible?* in the *Examine the Evidence* series).[2,11]

Archaeology Improves Bible Translation
(2 Kings 23:29)

Scholars were puzzled by the biblical (KJV) claim that Judah's King Josiah attacked Egypt's Pharaoh Neco, who "went *against* the king of Assyria." After all, at the time Assyria was an archenemy of Judah. But clay tablets found in the area indicated that Nineveh had already fallen, and Neco was going out to *"help"* Assyria. The Hebrew word could have meant either "against" or "help." Here, archaeology led to greater precision in recent Bible translations.[2]

King Jehoiachin—The evidence for Jehoiachin, who was king of Judah for only three months, then exiled to Babylon, is some of the most fascinating of all the kings. Three different jar handles have been found with an official seal of "Eliakim," a "steward of Jehoiachin" (in Beth Shemesh and Tell Beit Mirsim near Hebron). Even more interesting is a clay tablet "receipt" listing payment for rations of oil, barley, and other food to captives in Babylon, and listing King Jehoiachin and his five sons as recipients. The Bible describes how Evil-merodach, king of Babylon, brought Jehoiachin out of prison and gave him a daily allowance of food for the rest of his life (2 Kings 25:27-30).[2]

Nebuchadnezzar (Daniel 2–4)—Nebuchadnezzar (605–562 B.C.) is one of the most interesting people in the Bible. Hated for his cruel conquests and the deportation of the Jews, Nebuchadnezzar eventually repented and even wrote a chapter in the Bible (Daniel 4), something that few people realize. There is vast archaeological evidence of this ruler, who is known for his immense building projects. Excavations in Babylon document many of Nebuchadnezzar's building projects, including construction of some 20 temples and docks and expansion of the city's defenses. Many of the bricks taken from ancient sites even have the name of Nebuchadnezzar stamped on them. One excavated inscription reads, "The fortifications of Esagila and Babylon I strengthened and established the name of my reign forever." This statement reflects Nebuchadnezzar's similar boast recorded in the Bible (Daniel 4:30).[2]

Jeremiah's Prophecy (Jeremiah 42:8-12)—Jeremiah warned the Jewish leader Johanan (who was afraid of Nebuchadnezzar) *not* to go to Egypt (Jeremiah 42:19). When they took Jeremiah there anyway, the Lord gave the prophet instructions to hide stones in the brick pavement of an entrance to the palace of Tahpanhes, prophesying Nebuchadnezzar's future visit (Jeremiah 43:8-10).

Excavations at Tahpanhes uncovered this pavement, along with inscriptions that indicated it was never Nebuchadnezzar's plan to *conquer* Egypt—just to humble it.[2]

Ezekiel the Prophet (Book of Ezekiel)—Stone tablets have been uncovered in recent years that contain a nearly complete text of the Book of Ezekiel. Study of the specific form of Hebrew used in the inscriptions indicates the tablets were written during the time of Ezekiel—600 to 500 B.C. Some scholars have suggested they may have been chiseled by the prophet Ezekiel himself.[1]

The Return from Exile (Ezra, Haggai, Zechariah)—The Bible contains hundreds of fulfilled prophecies. Among the most amazing is the exile of the Jews and their return after 70 years (Jeremiah 25:9-11). It includes the very name of Cyrus, who would decree the return over 100 years future to the prediction (Isaiah 44:28). Irrefutable archaeological evidence provides confirmation of all these events, including the actual decree of Cyrus that the Jews return to rebuild the temple in 539 B.C. The Cyrus cylinder, found in Babylon, records this proclamation. Furthermore, it confirms other historical facts in the Bible, including the takeover of Babylon by the Persians without violence and the return of the treasures of the temple (Ezra 1:1-6).[1,2,12]

Susa (Sushan): City of Nehemiah (Nehemiah 1–2)—Nehemiah was cupbearer to Artaxerxes I in the Persian capital city of Susa when the king noticed his despair about the broken condition of the walls of Jerusalem. Artaxerxes not only granted Nehemiah permission to leave to rebuild the walls, but also provided him with goods and military support. This decree in 444 B.C. was a critical triggering of one of the most important prophecies in the Bible (Daniel 9:24-27): the prophecy predicting the precise day of Jesus' entry into Jerusalem on a donkey.[1] The city of Susa (also called Sushan) is located about 150 miles northeast of the top of the Persian Gulf. It has been under excavation longer than any other ancient city in Iran, with over 300 acres of area to work with. Included in the many finds are the Code of Hammurabi (see page 31) and the magnificent treasure-laden palace of Darius (the king before Xerxes and Artaxerxes I).[2]

Nehemiah, Sanballat, and Tobiah—The Elephantine papyri confirm many details about the Jews in Egypt and Palestine during the reign of Artaxerxes. Written only a generation after Nehemiah, they specifically refer to one of his adversaries: Sanballat, governor of Samaria, and his sons (Nehemiah 2:19; 4:1-3). Likewise, the Zeno papyri, discovered in Gerza (in Egypt), refer to Tobias, governor of Amman—a descendant of Nehemiah's adversary Tobiah the Ammonite (2:10).[2]

Drachmas: **Greek Coins**—Scholars once doubted the reference in Nehemiah regarding "drachmas" that were paid to the workers rebuilding the walls of Jerusalem (Nehemiah 7:70), believing that the Greek coins had not spread to Palestine by then. Excavations in Beth Zur, a few miles south of Jerusalem, uncovered several drachma coins from the Persian period—verifying the use of the coin in the area at the time of Nehemiah.[2]

Tyre: Fulfilled Prophecy—Although the Bible is silent between the Old and New Testament (400 B.C. to Jesus' time), archaeology continues to document fulfillment of many prophecies given earlier. Among them is the destruction in 586 B.C. of Tyre, the greatest seaport of Ezekiel's time (Ezekiel 26:3-16). Ezekiel prophesied that 1) Nebuchadnezzar would destroy the mainland city, 2) more than one nation would come against it, 3) it would be flattened like a bare rock, 4) it would be a site for spreading fishing nets, 5) the stones and timbers would be thrown into the waters, 6) the city would not be rebuilt, and 7) nearby rulers would give up their thrones. History has confirmed all of the prophecies. Perhaps the most unusual fulfillment came in 330 B.C., when Alexander the Great threw stones and timbers from the mainland city previously conquered by Nebuchadnezzar into the water to create a causeway to attack the city. So great was his victory that neighboring cities simply surrendered. Today, fisherman are seen drying nets on the bare, dry rock of the ancient city.

Josephus

Flavius Josephus (circa A.D. 37–100) was a prolific Jewish historian, whose multi-volume works about the Jewish people (most notably *Antiquities of the Jews*) cover Jewish history from the time of the book of Genesis and give confirming evidence of the Old Testament writings. However, Josephus is best known for his record of New Testament events, especially those that confirm the existence of Jesus, His miracles, John the Baptist, Jesus' brother James, and others.

Common Questions

What If I Don't Believe the Entire Bible?

Having a relationship with God does not depend on believing the entire Bible. Belief in and acceptance of Jesus as Savior are all that is required. Those who thoroughly investigate the Bible find abundant evidence that every claim of the Bible is true—and nearly all claims have substantial support. Even when "modern" science seems at odds with it, the Bible ultimately has proven true. But waiting to accept a relationship with Christ until *all* doubts are answered would be foolish. Your time on earth could end tomorrow. Instead, pray for insight. The truth will eventually be revealed.

How Can We Ensure the Right Relationship to Go to Heaven?

When Jesus said not all who use His name will enter heaven (Matthew 7:21–23), He was referring to people who think using Christ's name along with rituals and rules is the key to heaven. A *relationship* with God is *not* based on rituals and rules. It's based on grace and forgiveness, and the right kind of relationship with Him.

How to Have a Personal Relationship with God

1. **B**elieve that God exists and that He came to earth in the human form of Jesus Christ (John 3:16; Romans 10:9).

2. **A**ccept God's free forgiveness of sins through the death and resurrection of Jesus Christ (Ephesians 2:8-10; 1:7,8).

3. **S**witch to God's plan for life (1 Peter 1:21-23; Ephesians 2:1-5).

4. **E**xpress desire for Christ to be director of your life (Matthew 7:21-27; 1 John 4:15).

Prayer for Eternal Life with God

"Dear God, I believe You sent Your Son, Jesus, to die for my sins so I can be forgiven. I'm sorry for my sins, and I want to live the rest of my life the way You want me to. Please put Your Spirit in my life to direct me. Amen."

Then What?

People who sincerely take the above steps automatically become members of God's family of believers. A new world of freedom and strength is available through prayer and obedience to God's will. New members of God's family can build their relationship with God by taking the following steps:

- Find a Bible-based church that you like, and attend regularly.

- Try to set aside some time each day to pray and read the Bible.

- Locate other Christians to spend time with on a regular basis.

God's Promises to Believers

For Today

But seek first His kingdom and His righteousness,
and all these things [things to satisfy all your needs]
will be given to you as well.
—Matthew 6:33

For Eternity

Whoever believes in the Son has eternal life,
but whoever rejects the Son will not see life,
for God's wrath remains on him.
—John 3:36

Once we develop an eternal perspective, even the greatest problems on earth fade in significance.

Notes

1. Eastman, M.D., Mark and Missler, Chuck. *The Creator Beyond Time and Space*. Costa Mesa, CA: The Word for Today, 1996.

2. Free, Joseph P., and Vos, Howard F., *Archaeology and Bible History*. Grand Rapids, MI: Zondervan Publishing House, 1992.

3. *The Harper Atlas of the Bible*. New York: Harper & Row, 1987.

4. Jeffrey, Grant R. *The Signature of God*. Toronto, Ontario, Canada: Frontier Research Publications, 1996.

5. Josephus, Flavius. *The Complete Works of Josephus*. Grand Rapids, MI: Kregel Publications, 1981.

6. McDowell, Josh. *Evidence That Demands a Verdict—Volume II*. Nashville, TN: Thomas Nelson, Inc., 1993.

7. McDowell, Josh, and Wilson, Bill. *A Ready Defense*. San Bernardino, CA: Here's Life Publishers, Inc., 1990.

8. McRay, John. *Archaeology and the New Testament*. Grand Rapids, MI: Baker Book House, 1991.

9. Millard, Alan. *Illustrated Wonders and Discoveries of the Bible*. Nashville, TN: Thomas Nelson, Inc., 1997.

10. *Orange County Register*, August 6, 1993.

11. Shanks, Hershel, ed. *Understanding the Dead Sea Scrolls*. New York: Vintage Books, 1993.

12. Youngblood, Ronald F. *New Illustrated Bible Dictionary*. Nashville, TN: Nelson, 1995.

Bibliography

Archaeology and the Bible, The Best of BAR: Volume 1, Early Israel. Washington, DC: Bible Archaeology Society, 1990.

Encyclopedia Britannica. Chicago 1993.

Levi, Abraham and Ruth. *Bazak Guide to Israel*. New York: Harper Collins Publishers, 1993.

Life Application Bible. Wheaton, IL: Tyndale House Publishers, and Grand Rapids, MI: Zondervan Publishing House, 1991.

McDowell, Josh. *Evidence that Demands a Verdict—Volume I*. Nashville, TN: Thomas Nelson, Inc., 1979.

Muncaster, Ralph O. *Creation Versus Evolution—Investigation of the Evidence*. Mission Viejo, CA: Strong Basis to Believe, 1997.

Muncaster, Ralph O. *The Bible—Prophecy Miracles—Investigation of the Evidence*. Mission Viejo, CA: Strong Basis to Believe, 1996.

Muncaster, Ralph O. *The Bible—Scientific Insights—Investigation of the Evidence*. Mission Viejo, CA: Strong Basis to Believe, 1996.

Nelson's Complete Book of Bible Maps and Charts. Nashville, TN: Thomas Nelson, Inc., 1996.

Packer, J. I., and Tenney, Merrill C., and White, William Jr. *Illustrated Encyclopedia of Bible Facts*. Nashville, TN: Thomas Nelson, Inc., 1980.

Scott, Julius J., Ph.D. Life and Teachings of Jesus, audiotape. Wheaton, IL: Wheaton College Graduate School Extension Studies, 1988.

Smith, F. LaGard. The Daily Bible In Chronological Order. Eugene, OR: Harvest House, 1984.

Vos, Howard F. Introduction to Church History. Nashville, TN: Nelson, 1994.

What the Bible Is All About—Quick Reference Edition. Ventura, CA: Regal Books, 1989.

Who's Who in the Bible. Pleasantville, NY: Reader's Digest, 1994.